O9-BHL-254

ABC's of the Bible

CONTENTS

Welcome 2

ABC's of the Bible: An Introduction 3

Is It My Turn to Lead? 5

Racing the Clock 7

Session Schedule 9

Session 1:   Beginning the Scripture Journey 10

Session 2:   Taking the Next Step 22

Session 3:   Encountering a God of Love 32

Session 4:   Finding Faith and Hope 44

Session 5:   Embracing God and One Another 54

Session 6:   Continuing the Scripture Journey 66

Enriching the Experience 76

List of ABC Scriptures 78

Published by Christian Board of Publication, St. Louis, Missouri

Writer: Jon Berquist
Editor: Douglas D. Cripe
Series Editor: Michael E. Dixon

Art Director: Michael A. Domínguez
Cover design: Michael Foley
Interior design: Arista Graphics and Elizabeth Wright

Printed in the United States of America.

Visit our Web site: www.cbp21.com

FAITH CROSSINGS

WELCOME TO ABC'S OF THE BIBLE!

IF...

you are saying, "Help! I'm a leader! What do I do next?" go to pages 5–8.

you want to schedule the leaders and locations for this study, turn to page 9.

you're getting ready for the first meeting of your FAITH CROSS-INGS group and want to read Session 1 before you get there (always a good idea), look for page 10. Here you will begin the ABC adventure of learning about the Bible.

you want to discover unique activities to expand your FAITH CROSSINGS experience, check out "Enriching the Experience" on page 76.

you want to view all the ABC scriptures in this course, turn to page 78. You may photocopy these two pages to carry with you during the week.

ABC'S OF THE BIBLE

AN INTRODUCTION

"I've never really studied the Bible. I don't know the first thing about it."

"I try to read the Bible, but it's too confusing. I can't keep it all straight in my head."

"What is the Bible about anyway?"

"What is God like, and why do we even need the Bible to understand God?"

"Well, I can't even find the verses that people talk about unless someone tells me the page number."

If you've said any of these things—or thought them to yourself—this FAITH CROSSINGS course is for you.

In these sessions, you will begin to learn about the Bible, beginning with the basics of how to choose a translation or version of the Bible and how to find the verses. Throughout the sessions, you'll have a chance to read verses from the Bible, learn about what they originally meant, and talk with each other about how they can help your Christian life today. You won't learn everything about the Bible—but you'll start to learn how to study the Bible for yourself, and you'll learn enough of the background and context to help you in future Bible studies.

Years ago, children in Sunday school often learned memory verses. You may have done this yourself. One popular way to learn Bible verses was to learn one verse starting with each letter of the alphabet. Memory verses are not the best way for some adults to learn about the Bible, so that's not the primary focus of this study. We'll take twenty-six verses—one starting with each letter of the alphabet—as a way to begin discussion about a variety of verses and topics throughout the Bible. You do not have to memorize all the verses, although some people may want to. Some discover that committing specific verses to memory aids them later in life. In the midst of a crisis, memorized scripture can provide comfort and reassurance of God's great love.

In the twenty-six verses, we'll read parts of the whole Bible to get a taste of everything. Along the way, we'll learn some skills for Bible study and a little bit about the history of the Bible and God's activity in it. During this study, you'll encounter the major ideas and themes of the Bible. This should help you get a sense of the big picture, and every scripture passage after this should make more sense—whether it's another Bible study, a sermon, or anything else. The sessions are designed to be used with a Bible. Also, it's intended for use in a study group, where people have committed to work together to learn about the Bible. It's for beginners in Bible study—so jump right in!

IS IT MY TURN TO LEAD?

By Cathy Myers Wirt

Remember these leadership tips:

- ✓ **Read** the lesson more than once before leading it.
- ✓ Allow enough time to **gather materials or resources** you may need.
- ✓ **Pray** for the group members by name during the week.
- ✓ Create a **spirit of hospitality** and welcome in the meeting space through decoration, refreshments (if appropriate to your time), and name tags if needed.
- ✓ Offer brief gathering times for quick **sharing of news** of the congregation/group.
- ✓ If sensitive topics arise, agree on a policy of **confidentiality.** Stories told in a group should be shared outside of the group only when permission has been given.
- ✓ **Take all questions seriously** as a sign of the respect we hold for one another.
- ✓ If a person in the group has had a **tragedy** during the week, take time to deal with it even if it means delaying the session.
- ✓ **Direct** persons with serious emotional or spiritual dilemmas to the pastor.
- ✓ **Call persons who are absent** from the group during the week to check in on them and let them know that they have been missed.
- ✓ Encourage group members to **invite new people** to the group.
- ✓ **Ask for help** when you come across a topic or a problem in the group. You don't have to do this alone!
- ✓ **Allow silence** in the group while people think. Don't jump in too quickly to fill the quiet.
- ✓ Start and end the group with a **time of prayer.**
- ✓ Begin and end the session **on time.**

- ✓ **Vary your leading style** between thoughtful discussion, activity, and visual/auditory experiences. People learn in different ways.
- ✓ Connect the life of the group to the **congregation and the wider church.**
- ✓ **Watch the news media** for examples of the topics you are studying and bring in the articles for discussion and prayer.
- ✓ **Thank God** for the learning you are enjoying by leading the group. Leadership is one of the best ways to learn and increase your own faith.
- ✓ **Don't assume** that the people in the room know each other well.
- ✓ **Don't argue.** When strongly different opinions are expressed, try to avoid a win/lose style of discussion.
- ✓ **Invite but don't coerce people to discuss.** Some people learn by listening and may be fully attentive without speaking.
- ✓ Help keep one from **monopolizing the discussion.** Pass the discussion to another person by saying, "[name], what do you think about this idea/story?" Try always to do this in love.
- ✓ **Avoid getting sidetracked** by talking about people not in the room. Try to keep the discussion on the experiences and ideas of those in the room.
- ✓ **Avoid becoming unfocused** on the session. A group that has spun into other topics can be brought back by statements like, "What in the session reminded you of that?" or "Wow, how did we get to this topic from today's lesson?" or "What you just said reminded me about our lesson today because…"

RACING THE CLOCK
A Leader's Guide to Getting through a Session

A typical FAITH CROSSINGS session gives more activities than time may allow. That's good news—there's a lot to choose from; and bad news—how do you choose? That depends. When you're leading a group of adults, there are a lot of variables! An activity that may take five minutes for one group may lead to a twenty-minute discussion in another. With all that in mind, here are some suggestions.

- ▲ Encourage everyone to read "Before the Session" before arriving. This section provides continuity and background to help the group members start "on the same page." Then the leader doesn't have to take time to summarize the information.

- ▲ In most cases, each session has four basic movements, each beginning with the phrase "Connecting with…" Be sure that you spend some time with each movement. (See the paragraph below on how to adapt this flow to a forty-five-minute church school session.)

- ▲ Note the key activities. 🔑 This logo after the title of an activity is your clue that it is essential to the session. If you don't have enough time to cover everything, be sure you cover the key activities.

- ▲ Pick and choose from the remaining activities, according to your interests and the interests of the group. If your group doesn't like an arts-based activity, for example, that may be a good one to draw a big X through before the session even begins.

- ▲ Go with the flow. Don't let agenda anxiety put a premature end to a really great discussion. And don't drag out an activity that people aren't responding to—just summarize and move on.

Adapting to a church school setting

Each session is written for a ninety-minute group setting. If you want to use it in church school, how do you adapt? Two suggestions:

1. Allow twelve weeks for the six sessions. During the first week of a given session, cover what you can and close with a prayer. When the next week's session begins, summarize what the group covered the first week. Then work through the remaining activities.

2. Lead one session a week for six weeks. If you do this, there will probably be time for little more than the key activities. Highlight some of the important discussion questions you wish to include from the other activities. Encourage the group members to read the whole session, but select those activities for group use that connect to your particular group.

SESSION SCHEDULE

Session 1
When _____ Leader _____
Where _____

Session 2
When _____ Leader _____
Where _____

Session 3
When _____ Leader _____
Where _____

Session 4
When _____ Leader _____
Where _____

Session 5
When _____ Leader _____
Where _____

Session 6
When _____ Leader _____
Where _____

Special Activities
When _____ Leader _____
Where _____

1

Beginning the Scripture Journey

(A through D)

Session Focus: From hymns of faith to stories about Jesus, the Bible contains a variety of books. In one of these writings, we hear Jesus invite us to treat others as we want them to treat us.

Focus Scriptures: Joshua 24:15b; Psalm 51; Matthew 5:1–12; Luke 6:20–49

BEFORE THE SESSION

To see the scope of the many translations that exist, visit the American Bible Society on line at www.american bible.org.

Bibles come in many different versions. Although there are hundreds in English from which to choose, there are about a dozen common ones. Use the Bible version with which you feel comfortable. If you do not have a favorite, ask other people to recommend their favorites. If several different versions exist in the group, members can hear the differences that occur in translations. Sometimes a slightly different word can bring a whole new meaning to a Bible verse.

When this study refers to specific verses, it will usually be from the *New Revised Standard Version.* This contemporary version offers a good balance between accuracy in the translation and readability in the style. The *New International Version* also provides another option. For many people, the favorites are the *King James Version* or the *New King James Version*. These translations are beautiful in a very formal way. The *New King James Version* is more accurate than the old one since the original *King James Version* is nearly 400 years old, more like Shakespeare than the way people write and talk today. The *New American Standard Bible* is also very formal; it is extremely accurate but not very easy to read. The *New Jerusalem Bible* and the *Revised English Bible* are not as common but are also good choices. The *Good News Bible* (sometimes called *Today's English Version*) and the *Living Bible* are readable, but sometimes not as accurate as the others. If you use these latter versions, be sure to compare to other translations from time to time. A new and readable version is the *Contemporary English Version*, an excellent translation that uses easy-to-understand language for today's listeners.

For information about the *Access Bible*, a recent NRSV Bible from Oxford University Press, visit www.accessbible.com.

CONNECTING WITH ONE ANOTHER

1. Encounter the Bible

The Bible is a beautiful book filled with the truths of our faith. It's also a very scary book. It can be hard to understand, much longer and more difficult than almost anything else we are used to reading, and it is so old that at times it's hard to figure out what it means and how it's relevant. And there's one other problem: Because it's so important to faith, a lot of people are afraid to admit that they don't know much of the Bible or that they find it hard to read.

It's OK to admit your unfamiliarity with the Bible, for this is a study for people who are just starting out reading the Bible. You are not expected to know everything now. This study will start at the beginning, and the first thing we'll learn is how to find different parts within the Bible. Stop and ask questions at any time. Maybe someone can help you find the answer. Probably other people have the same question. If no

Tell one
another what
the Bible means
to you or how it
impacts your life.

one in the group knows the answer, you can always find someone who can help, such as another teacher or minister in your congregation.

What does the Bible mean to you? Maybe you have a memory verse from childhood that you still remember. Is there a special Bible that has been in your family or that you received as a gift? Maybe you have a funny story—those are OK, too. If this is your first time to see and hold a Bible, say that. Everyone starts somewhere!

2. Compare translations

Compare several
scripture passages
from various
translations.

As mentioned in "Before the Session," many different Bible translations have been written throughout the centuries. The original Hebrew and Greek languages have been translated into thousands of languages and dialects. How did you begin using the translation you use? What other translations do members of the group use? How does Psalm 51:10 or Matthew 5:3, for example, sound in different translations?

CONNECTING WITH THE THEME

3. Examine the Bible structure

"As for me and my household, we will serve the LORD."
(Joshua 24:15b)

The first step in any study of scripture is to find the verses to read and discuss. For most of history, it has been difficult to find a specific verse within the Bible. After all, it is a big book, and it can be hard to find your way around in it. People would memorize long passages of scripture. If someone else referred to a scripture, people would have to pull it out of their memories. Or, they would refer to the first few words on a page or the first line of a passage; that was the only way to find a scripture so that everyone could read or hear the verses.

But for the last few hundred years, there has been a more convenient way. When one person divided the books of the Bible into chapters, divided the chapters into verses, and numbered both the chapters and the verses, it became much easier to find a passage. Each scripture is located within a book, a chapter, and a verse. Genesis, Exodus, Matthew, and Mark, for example, are all books. Some of the books are so closely connected that they have numbers in front: 1 Samuel (or First Samuel) and 2 Samuel (or Second Samuel) are parts of the same story.

Find the Old and New Testaments in the Bible.

In addition, the Bible is divided into two big sections, usually called the Old Testament and the New Testament. Sometimes the Old Testament is called the First Testament, or the Hebrew Bible or Hebrew Scriptures because it was mostly written in Hebrew. The New Testament is sometimes called the Second Testament. The Old Testament is about twenty to twenty-two centuries old, and the New Testament is about eighteen centuries old—it may be newer, but it's hardly new.

The quickest way to find a specific book is also the hardest—memorize in order the names of the thirty-nine books of the Old Testament and the twenty-seven books of the New Testament. The books are not arranged alphabetically or chronologically, but there are some thematic groupings. Memorization can help you understand some important things about the content of scripture. But there are easier ways. Some Bibles have tabs on the sides of the pages. And almost every Bible has a table of contents and page numbers. There's nothing wrong in using those tools.

Find the table of contents.

Find Joshua 24:15b in your own Bible.

For this scripture, Joshua 24:15b, the reference means that this is the book of Joshua, chapter 24, verse 15 of that chapter. When you find the book of Joshua, find the twenty-fourth chapter and look down the verses to the fifteenth. The letter *b* in verse 15b means that the sentence quoted is the second half of the verse; if it were *a* it would refer to the first half of the verse.

Locate
examples
of these smaller
books.

There are a few exceptions to this system of numbering chapters and verses. Some biblical books are so short that they aren't separated into chapters. These books include Obadiah, Philemon, 2 John, 3 John, and Jude. In these cases, Obadiah 3 means the third *verse* of the book of Obadiah, not the third *chapter*.

The chapter and verse system makes it easier for people to find verses, but a danger exists in this system. We may sometimes view a verse as a separate unit, something independent. In the Bible, just like in any book, context is very important. You need to read what's around the verse in order to make sense of it.

How do you
proclaim your
faithfulness
to God?

In the case of Joshua 24:15b, the chapter provides a context of a ceremony, a huge public event in which Joshua, the leader of the Israelites, makes an announcement of his commitment to follow God. Immediately before this scripture in verse 14, Joshua talks about choosing to follow God and to stop following other gods. To proclaim faithfulness to God is to give up something, because it requires denying all the other forces and priorities that could lay claim to one's life.

4. Explore a Gospel

"*B*lessed are the poor in spirit, for theirs is the kingdom of heaven." (Matthew 5:3)

Find the four
Gospels.

The New Testament contains four books that tell stories of Jesus. These books are called gospels. *Gospel* means "good news," and these four books contain the early church's memories of Jesus, told to explain their claim that Jesus is God's good news for all people.

Find Matthew 5.

Matthew is the first gospel and begins the New Testament. The beginning of Matthew 5 contains one of Jesus' best known teachings, often called the Beatitudes. This passage is a presentation of ethics, a set of nine sentences about the principles by which Christians should live their lives. It is part of a larger set of Jesus' teachings, called the Sermon on the Mount, which continues for several chapters.

Which Beatitudes relate to how you live your life?

No one knows what it was like to listen to Jesus teach and preach. The gospels tell many of Jesus' teachings, but also warn us there are more things he said than have been preserved. If you read any one of the four gospels from start to finish, you might get the impression that Jesus gave several carefully crafted sermons over the space of several years, never repeating himself. But it is much more likely that Jesus offered similar ideas and teachings many times. Perhaps he gave the same sermon in each town, or perhaps each one contained many of the same ideas but were expressed in different words. The gospels do not record every sermon in a word-for-word fashion. Instead, Jesus' teachings in the gospels are collections and summaries of what Jesus said, as remembered, told, recorded, preserved, and explained by a generation or two of the earliest Christians after Jesus and before the gospels were written.

5. Encounter a psalm 🔑

Find the Psalms quickly by opening your Bible near the middle.

"Create in me a clean heart, O God, and put a new and right spirit within me." (Psalm 51:10)

For many Christians, the Psalms are one of the favorite parts of the Old Testament. This beautiful set of poems expresses a variety of emotions and ideas. Many of them are highly evocative reflections on faith, sometimes in the form of an intimate prayer between a believer and God.

Because these psalms can seem so personal and individual, it is easy to neglect the questions of why they were written and how they were used. Asking these kinds of historical questions can feel like violating the intention of the emotionally vibrant poetry of the psalms. But we must pay attention to the history of writing and use in any biblical material. Deep down, it's a matter of respect. When you write something, you want it to be used in a way that's consistent with the way it was written. For the same reason, we should be careful that we use scripture in faithful ways.

In a modern society, people are surrounded with words. Everywhere we go we meet requests to become readers. From the time the morning paper arrives, we read. If we drive or take public transportation, signs tell us what to do and how to drive. Our mail—whether postal mail or e-mail—contains words waiting to be read. Even if you pick up the phone to escape the written word, you might look in a phone book to find the number. At work we encounter manuals or computers; at home we read tags, recipes, or instructions on packages. At the end of the day we pick up a novel or a magazine to unwind.

All these words come in packages called texts, and there are rules and conventions for how to read different kinds of texts. You not only need to know the language to be a successful reader; you have to know the cultural conventions in order to know how to make sense of each text. A love letter and a phone book are both wonderful things to have—but they do very different things. Having one when you need the other isn't much help, and there are differences in how you read them. One you read start to finish, concentrating on each word; the other you keep around and read a line at a time when you need it. It's a silly example, but it's a crucial point. Each text is one of a category of texts (the categories are sometimes called genres [ZHAN-rah] or forms), and each has its own rules.

Psalms are part of a category of worship materials. They were written as poetry or hymns to read or

On a dry erase board, chalkboard, or newsprint, list the various types of texts you encounter in a day.

sing in ancient temple worship services. When we read them ourselves, silently and privately, we use them in a different setting. The psalms still have value, but we must remember their original context.

Locate Psalm 51.

Psalm 51:10 comes from the middle of the chapter, but look at the first line: "Have mercy on me, O God." This is a prayer! And like any letter or conversation, it's meant to be read start-to-finish, without taking a line out of the middle, out of context. In this psalm is a plea to God to forgive sin. The sin is never named; it doesn't need to be, because this is a prayer for everyone in worship. But forgiveness takes more than prayer. In the middle of this passage, the person praying asks God to create a clean heart and a new spirit (v. 10). It takes God's action to complete the act of forgiveness, so that the joy of being someone whom God has saved returns (v. 12). Forgiveness never comes easily; it is a process that requires newness and dedication to a larger cause.

When have you prayed this type of prayer?

Because of this need, the psalm does not end here. The one praying promises to teach God's ways to others, to praise God out loud, and even to build God's society in concrete ways (v. 13–19). Forgiveness means a new spirit, and this changes lives.

6. Read more of Jesus' teachings

"Do to others as you would have them do to you." (Luke 6:31)

Luke 6:20–49 presents several of Jesus' sayings, a collection of ideas Jesus frequently used in his preaching. Matthew, Mark, Luke, and John all recount Jesus' actions and speeches in a rough chronological order. Of these, Mark is the shortest and probably the oldest. Matthew and Luke each use some of Mark's material, but they add other stories and speeches. Matthew often focuses more interest on Jewish practices of the time, and Luke recounts more stories of women who interacted with Jesus.

Sometimes, Matthew and Luke agree on the details of stories with Mark; sometimes they differ. John tells a very different story and contains information that the other three gospels do not mention. The other three gospels are called "Synoptic Gospels," which means they share much of the same viewpoint on Jesus, when compared with the Gospel of John.

Many people would have experienced parts of Jesus' life, ministry, and preaching, but most of them would have seen and heard only fragments. Soon many Christians existed who had never even met Jesus. They only knew what others told them. Over many decades, thousands of stories about Jesus circulated. Dozens of complete books were written to present the "whole story" of Jesus, although none of these books were really the whole story. They each had their own interests and emphases, and they told different stories from their distinct viewpoints. Out of all these early gospels, only four became part of the church's traditional New Testament: Matthew, Mark, Luke, and John.

Matthew tells of Jesus preaching on a hillside, and this is sometimes known as the Sermon on the Mount (Matthew 5—8). It's one of the most extensive summaries of Jesus' teaching available in the gospels. Luke's Gospel has many of the same teachings and preaching, but in a different style, in Luke 6:20–49. Sometimes we call this the sermon on the plain, since Luke says Jesus taught these things while in a level place, instead of on a mountain where Matthew says Jesus taught these things. This minor difference is not very significant, since Jesus certainly taught a variety of things in many places.

Compare Matthew's hillside sermon with Luke's sermon on the plain.

7. Live Jesus' teachings 🔑

In Luke, Jesus provides an ethical code that is far from easy. The phrase "do unto others as you would

CONNECTING WITH LIFE

ABC's of the Bible

have them do to you" sounds nicer without all the specifics that Jesus speaks around it. Set in the larger context of this sermon's ethical demands, we see that following Jesus is going to be very difficult. It requires a change in how we live our lives.

When have you experienced someone treating you like you wanted, instead of like you deserved—or worse? How can we treat others like we want to be treated? What will happen when we love our enemies? What changes in our lives will we have to make to love our enemies?

8. Identify blessings in our lives

Two of the scriptures in this session are set in the context of Jesus' memorable teaching about blessings. Some of what makes a saying of Jesus memorable is not just the content, but also the way it is expressed. Often, the New Testament quotes Jesus speaking in very easy-to-remember expressions and formulas. The Beatitudes are one example of this, with their pattern of "Blessed are the...for they are..."

What do these sayings mean? Today, when we talk about "blessings" we usually mean positive things that happen to us. When a family adds a newborn child in good health, people call it a blessing. A good-paying job is a blessing. A recovery from a difficult surgery—or a report of clean health—is considered a blessing. In our increasingly consumerist society, sometimes we will call something a blessing when it's really nothing more than a purchase, such as a new car or an expensive vacation. But these ideas about blessings seem very far away from what Jesus teaches.

Blessed people, according to Jesus, are merciful, pure, peaceful, meek, and poor; they desire justice and they experience persecution as their only reward. In what way are these blessings? Clearly, Jesus

Discuss the listed questions about Jesus' ethical code and how we can live out his teachings in our lives.

Name times you have heard people refer to blessings in their lives. How do they compare to the blessings Jesus named?

Discuss: When have you felt blessed? When have you felt the things that Jesus talks about as blessings? What would the world be like if we followed Jesus' ideas about who is blessed?

has different ideas than we do. Jesus points the way to a very different kind of life.

9. Envision God's hope for the world

Review the four scripture verses in this session. From these four verses, what can you discern about how God wants the world to be? How can Christians work together for this kind of world? What can members of the group do individually or together to bring about God's vision for the world?

Before the next session, you may want to try to memorize the four key verses for this session. If you work on one every other day, you can get through these in a week. These memory verses can remind you throughout the week about God's vision for the world.

See Activity 1 on page 76 to make cards as an aid in memorization.

On the next page, jot down notes during the week about how the four verses in this session influence you.

10. Pray for one another

Pray each line of the following prayer, allowing silence for members to add specific prayer concerns between the lines.

Our God, we thank you for speaking to us through your Spirit and through scripture.

Help us to commit ourselves to following you and to serving you. Make us your partners in this world and turn our thoughts from all others whom we could serve instead.

Teach us what it means to be truly blessed. Help us to live life according to your values.

Give us clean hearts and right spirits, so that we can understand your desires for our lives.

Work with us so that we love our enemies.

In all things, our God, keep us close to you and one another and help us to learn from you and from your scriptures. Amen.

NOTES

2

Taking the Next Step
(E through H)

Session Focus: Jesus invites us to discover God's eternal love and to follow him as disciples. As followers of Jesus, God calls us to care for those in need and proclaim the good news of Jesus Christ to all the world.

Focus Scriptures: 2 Corinthians 9:7; John 3:16; Matthew 28:19–20; Deuteronomy 6:4–5

BEFORE THE SESSION

Compare the similarities and differences between your congregation and a group of early Christians.

Think about what it would have been like to be a Christian in the first century. In many towns there might be only a dozen or less people meeting in small groups. The largest gatherings were almost certainly less than fifty people, except for the Christians in Jerusalem. These small groups would typically meet in someone's house to talk about their faith, to remember stories of Jesus, and to share news with one another.

One big difference between the early Christians and us is that we have the New Testament and they did not. The first books of the New Testament probably came fifteen years after Jesus. Other books were still being written sixty years or more after Jesus. Christians in these early years did not have all the New Testament books on which to base their faith. Instead, they had the stories they told one another. Also, they had the scriptures that we now call the Old Testament, and they read those to one another regularly.

These small Christian groups would have included a variety of people. The New Testament tells us of rich people and slaves who were members of the same worshiping group, along with Jews and people of every nation, different races, people who grew up in different religions, people who disagreed with each other strongly, families and single persons, men and women, young and old. All of them gathered and ate a meal as they shared their lives and their faith. Over time, these groups became very close-knit. They were not perfect; we can be certain that they experienced petty bickering. But they were united in their love of God and Jesus and their love for one another.

1. Identify favorite stories of the Bible

Some people have a favorite book or story from the Bible. Others find meaning in a particular verse or character. At points in our lives, we may identify with a particular character or story in relation to the events of our lives. For example, someone falsely accused of a crime may identify with Joseph when Potiphar's wife accused him of trying to seduce her. (See Genesis 39.) Even adults who do not feel they know the Bible very well may recall stories from their early years that carry meaning.

2. Recall the previous verses 🔑

Review or recall last session's verses, A through D. Which ones did you recall? Which verses came to mind during the past week? What do they mean to you now? How did they change your attitude or your actions? How did they remind you of God's vision for the world?

CONNECTING WITH ONE ANOTHER

Discuss: What biblical story seems to speak to you? What do you like about it?

Invite the group members to recite what they remember from the four verses from the last session. Use the list on page 78 or create a large display of verses on newsprint. If they cannot recite them, ask them to recall what the passages were about.

3. Celebrate your giving

"Each of you must give as you have made up your mind, not reluctantly or under compulsion, for God loves a cheerful giver." (2 Corinthians 9:7)

After Jesus' life and death the disciples saw Jesus again for several weeks, and they announced that Jesus had been brought back to life through resurrection. The story of Jesus and his followers did not end with Jesus' death. After less than two months, they saw Jesus returning to heaven. After that the sightings of Jesus were extremely rare.

Even when Jesus stopped appearing, the story was not over. Jesus' followers continued to meet, and they kept alive the memory of Jesus' teachings. These early Christians spread through other parts of the Roman Empire (around the Mediterranean Sea in Europe, Asia Minor, and North Africa), a tiny minority in the midst of a world that had many religions. In many towns, there may have been only one or two dozen Christians. Because the Christians were spread out among many towns, it was a challenge to stay in touch with other Christians.

Paul (also known as Saul) was one of the early Christian leaders who began his ministry after all Gospel events ended. Much of his work focused on keeping the early Christians connected to one another. He traveled frequently among the Christian gatherings in different towns. He preached and taught, and he learned from other Christians and passed the stories and beliefs of one Christian group to another.

Skim the stories of Paul in Acts 7:54—8:3 and 9:1–31, as well as Acts 13—28.

Like many other early leaders, Paul wrote letters to many churches, and the New Testament preserved several of these letters. Paul wrote to the church in the city of Corinth. First and Second Corinthians contain parts of his letters, but we do not know what the church in Corinth had written to Paul. When he answers their questions in his letter, we may get

ABC's of the Bible

Read 2 Corinthians 9:7. Do you give reluctantly or cheerfully? How does your attitude make a difference?

Discuss: How do members of your congregation care for one another? How does your congregation respond to people who are suffering?

confused since we hear only one part of the conversation.

When Paul wrote the letter that became Second Corinthians, the Christians in Jerusalem were suffering. They were having trouble affording enough food to eat, and so Paul encouraged Christians from other cities to collect an offering to provide them aid. Giving is important for Christians, because part of what it means to be Christian is to care for one another. When others hurt, we help them, whether or not we know them personally. Christians must stay connected to one another, with deep concern for the lives of other Christians near and far.

4. Discover God's eternal love 🗝

"For God so loved the world that he gave his only Son, so that everyone who believes in him may not perish but may have eternal life." (John 3:16)

No verse of scripture is more well-known—or well-loved—than this one. Many Christians in a variety of denominations, beliefs, and perspectives find that this verse expresses the essence of the gospel.

In the last session we saw how different gospels told the story of Jesus in different ways, with different concerns and issues and emphasizing different viewpoints. The Gospel of John is the one of the four gospels that is most unlike the others. John records many stories and sayings of Jesus not found in Matthew, Mark, or Luke. In the other three gospels (called the Synoptic Gospels), Jesus does not speak openly of who he is or why he is sent until later in the story, and sometimes it seems that Jesus discovers his mission and purpose as the story goes. Even when Jesus and others say plainly that Jesus is the Son of God, Jesus warns them not to tell anyone.

In the Gospel of John, however, Jesus knows from the beginning who he is, and he begins to explain it to people right from the start. In chapter 3, Jesus is talking with Nicodemus, a faithful person who asks Jesus questions in order to learn who Jesus is. Jesus talks about God, and soon Nicodemus seems unable to handle all this theological insight. He asks Jesus, "How can these things be?" (3:9). Jesus announces that he is the Son of Man, descended from heaven to bring heavenly truths to humanity.

Jesus refers to an old story about Moses, one of the most famous leaders of the Israelite people, as told in Numbers 21:6–9. The people of Israel were complaining because they did not believe God was taking care of them very well, and so God sent poisonous snakes to bite them. When the people started dying from snakebites, Moses prayed to God, and God offered a way to save them: Moses would make a bronze snake and lift it up on a pole so that everyone could see it. God promised that anyone who would look upon the bronze snake would live. Jesus explains that he is like that bronze snake; Jesus would be lifted up in a death of crucifixion, like a snake on a pole, so that God could save those who looked at Jesus in the belief that God could save.

The early Christians who heard this story of Jesus may have felt like they were surrounded by snakes of all kinds, including powerful people who were part of other religions who persecuted Christians for their beliefs. But in the midst of those persecutions, this story reminded the early Christians that God gave them Jesus to save them. If we look at Jesus and believe, then God will save us—not from snakebites, but by teaching us the truth so that we can do what is right.

Christians in the centuries since this gospel was first written have heard something vital about Jesus as well. According to the gospels, Jesus is God's clearest way of showing humanity how much God loves us. God loves us so much that God will stop at nothing to provide for us ways to find our salvation, our

ABC's of the Bible

Discuss: What is
eternal life like?
How do you
know? When
have you experi-
enced new life?
How does your
experience relate
to the things
the group listed
earlier? What
helped bring
about the
change?

Whom do you
know that needs
to be saved, but
that you have a
hard time loving?

ability to judge correctly what is right for us to do, and the opportunity to live fully and deeply. Everyone who believes in Jesus will have eternal life. This is not just life after death, but a different kind of life now. This eternal life is life with God on a daily basis, with nothing to hide.

This is also a verse about how much God loves the world, not just about God's love for Christians and believers. God loves the sinners, the condemned, and those who act in poor judgment and have some- thing to hide—just as God loved the snakebitten complainers in the story of Moses. God will not stop at anything, not even the giving of God's son Jesus, until the whole world knows that love.

5. Be disciples

"Go therefore and make disciples of all nations, baptizing them in the name of the Father and of the Son and of the Holy Spirit, and teaching them to obey everything that I have com- manded you. And remember, I am with you always, to the end of the age." (Matthew 28:19–20)

This verse comes at the very end of the Gospel of Matthew. After Jesus' death, the disciples started see- ing Jesus again, having discovered that Jesus' tomb was empty. In Matthew's Gospel, these appearances are for Jesus' closest followers only, and the leaders of Jerusalem circulate the story that the disciples stole Jesus' body from the tomb by night. In the final scene of the gospel, Jesus appears to the eleven disci- ples. The sight of Jesus raised to life was so amazing that not even the disciples believed their eyes. Jesus gave them the charge in this verse, to go into the world and make more disciples.

Early in the gospel stories, Jesus calls people to follow him and to listen to his teachings. Over time, twelve men accept Jesus' invitation. Some of these twelve followers seem to be with Jesus all the time. Some are familiar names, such as Peter, John, and

Discuss: What
does it mean to be
a disciple of Jesus?

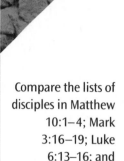

Compare the lists of disciples in Matthew 10:1–4; Mark 3:16–19; Luke 6:13–16; and Acts 1:13.

Judas. Others are never mentioned again in the gospels or in Acts, and nothing is known of what they did. In Matthew 10:1–4 and Mark 3:16–19, Jesus selects these twelve as apostles. An *apostle* is someone who is "sent out" to take care of a task somewhere else. What makes these twelve special is the task that Jesus gives them, which is to preach the good news of God's love and God's reign and to cure illnesses and care for people.

Many others in the gospels follow Jesus, too. The gospels name Mary Magdalene, Joanna, and Mary the mother of James (Luke 24:10), for instance. Mary, Martha, and Lazarus are followers and friends of Jesus in the Gospel of John. Many of the people whom Jesus healed and some of those who heard him teach chose to follow him.

At the end of the Gospel of Matthew, Jesus gathers the eleven disciples (Judas killed himself after selling information about Jesus' location) and directs them to go and make more disciples everywhere in the whole world. Now everyone is to be a disciple.

So what are the disciples like? They carry on the tasks that they had been given originally: to announce God's love and reign and to care for the sick and other hurting people. Instead of doing this only in their own neighborhoods, they must now do this throughout the whole world, to the ends of the earth. Now they have two new tasks: to initiate people into the church through baptism and to teach others what they have heard from Jesus.

Followers of Jesus, who were first called disciples and then only later given the name of Christian, are those who tell the world of God's love and who make that love real through their actions of care for individuals in need. Christian care means giving to the world, not just to other Christians. The gifts of health and love and concern and care do not come after the preaching of the good news—caring for

ABC's of the Bible

others is the good news, and God's love takes human form in our hands.

6. Hear God's teachings

"Hear, O Israel: The Lord is our God, the Lord alone. You shall love the Lord your God with all your heart, and with all your soul, and with all your might." (Deuteronomy 6:4–5)

These verses form the heart of Jewish faith today, as they have for thousands of years. The word *hear* in Hebrew is *shema* (sh-MAH), and so this passage is often called the Shema.

An old legend says that experts in the Jewish religious traditions of Jesus' time were required to learn over six hundred instructions of the faith. Students would be tested on every law until they were all memorized exactly. For the final exam, a student had to recite the important parts of the law, the essence of faith, from memory—while standing on one foot. Some would try the Ten Commandments or some other combination of essential statements of the faith. If Jesus were to take this final exam on the Jewish faith, his answer would start with the Shema, for there is nothing more central about how we should respond to the good news than to love God completely.

Read Mark 12:28–31 and compare to Leviticus 19:18.

When a scribe asked Jesus to explain what was the most important law, he began with the Shema and added a law from Leviticus that referred to love for one's neighbor. In the context of Leviticus (the third book of the Old Testament, which contains a number of specific instructions of the law), it's clear that the neighbor doesn't just mean the person who lives in the apartment or house next to you. It means everyone you meet. Jesus even tells a story (often called the parable of the good Samaritan, in Luke 10:25–37) about this. Foreigners, people in pain, victims, and others are neighbors to us, and they are the ones we should love.

If all we had were the commandments from Deuteronomy and Leviticus, how would life be different? How would we act if these were the most important things in our lives?

7. Recognize our limits

Jesus told the disciples to go into the world teaching about God's love, and the apostle Paul requested the church in Corinth to collect money for believers in Jerusalem. Being a disciple and following Jesus involves helping others, but sometimes this is not always easy and we may fail.

Being disciples doesn't mean we're perfect. Many of the disciples failed. Often the disciples were the slowest ones to recognize who Jesus was. Peter denied Jesus, and Judas betrayed him, yet they were both disciples. We are imperfect, like these first disciples of Christ. We, too, will deny and even betray Jesus, but we will still be disciples, even when we fail. Discipleship is not about being flawless; it is about being in love with the world, just as God so loved the world.

8. Help a neighbor

Think about a neighbor of yours—whether it's someone who lives near you, someone at work or school, someone you see regularly, a family member, a friend, or a stranger. Ask yourself how you will make God's love real to that person in the week ahead. How does the biblical story help you make God's love real to others? How does the Bible assist you in communicating God's love to others? How could a verse or story from this session help another person come to recognize God's care?

9. Pray together

Our God, we thank you for loving us so much
that you sent your Son, Jesus.
Teach us to love you with our whole hearts.
Teach us to love our neighbors as you have loved us.
Show us how to stretch out our hands to help the
world,
and to show your love to everyone, near and far.

Amen.

Discuss:
How does your congregation deal with imperfect disciples? How do people respond when someone misses meetings, forgets to do a task, or yells at someone in a disagreement? What do you do when you don't feel you have the energy to be a disciple in the way the church expects us to be?

CONNECTING WITH GOD

Invite group members to tell of times they have referred to stories in the Bible or read scripture to help other people find God's love or struggle through a crisis.

Pray the prayer in unison.

NOTES

3

Encountering a God of Love

(I through M)

Session Focus: From exploring the beginnings of the world to encountering Mary's words of joy and Jesus' tears of sorrow, the Bible shows us a God of love. God's wisdom provides a vision that all creation can encounter this love.

Focus Scriptures: Genesis 1:1–3; John 11:35; Proverbs 4:26; Philippians 2:4; Luke 1:46–47

BEFORE THE SESSION

In the past sessions we have seen stories of Jesus in the gospels, emotional poetry in the psalms, letters written to early Christian congregations, prayers, sermons that Jesus preached, and summaries of the ancient law. These are only some of the things found in scripture. The Bible has a little of almost everything!

One needs to know where to look for certain kinds of writing, but that can be a problem. The books of the Bible are not in chronological order or in a thematic arrangement, so it often feels like the Bible is not arranged in a user-friendly way.

As you spend time reading the Bible, the connections become more apparent, and you can learn the location of different writings. Even if you do not know from memory the location of a specific verse, you'll get better at figuring out where to look.

Tools exist that can help you find things in the Bible. Sometimes you know a specific word you want to find. In that case, you need a concordance. Concordances list the words in the Bible in alphabetical order and list the scripture references where those words appear. Look for one in your church or city library. Software concordances for computers can help you find words in the Bible quickly.

Sometimes you do not know a specific word but only the general topic, or you have found a word in scripture but do not know what it means. In that case, use a Bible dictionary, such as *The HarperCollins Bible Dictionary* (edited by Paul Achtemeier) and the *Mercer Dictionary of the Bible* (edited by Watson Mills). Both are relatively recent and contain a lot of reliable information. Many church and public libraries will have one of them. You can look up a topic and find a short discussion of different scripture passages.

When you look for something in scripture, examine the whole context. An easy mistake in reading scripture occurs when you find a single verse that appears to answer your question—and then stop without further investigation. When you read the Bible, read before and after the verse to get a sense of the context of the surrounding story. Remember that each verse of the Bible was written to other people a long time ago; it was not written only to answer the question you happen to have today.

CONNECTING WITH ONE ANOTHER

Invite members to discuss their memorization. Take turns recalling the verses from the past two sessions.

1. Check on memorization

At the start of the session, talk with each other about your attempts to memorize these key verses. Do not be discouraged; memorization is hard work, and it is not for everyone. If you have trouble memorizing the verses, think together about other ways you can learn the meaning of them. Perhaps you can make note cards with the verses and read them to yourself once or twice a day.

2. Recall previous scriptures

The previous session encouraged you to think how scripture can reflect God's love to others. How did the verses from the previous session remind you of God's care this past week? In what context were you able to tell others about your faith? How did you make God's love real this week? How did the Bible assist you or not assist you in this process? When is it not appropriate to quote scripture to someone?

3. Explore beginnings

"In the beginning when God created the heavens and the earth, the earth was a formless void and darkness covered the face of the deep, while a wind from God swept over the face of the waters. Then God said, 'Let there be light'; and there was light." (Genesis 1:1–3)

Almost every human culture wonders how the world began. In modern Western culture, questions about how things started often receive technical, scientific answers. The theories of the Big Bang and evolution are widely accepted in this culture. Simplistically, they say space and time, including the material that became stars, the dust that became planets, and even the matter that eventually became life on earth, began as a huge, hot mass which exploded. As the matter sped away from the center, it began to slow down and cool. The shapeless matter settled into patterns, and eventually these patterns became stars, planets, and everything else in the cosmos. Each planet consisted of materials and chemicals, and some of these combined in ways that could copy itself into new generations; this is what we call life. Living creatures, from plants to animals to the mammal we call human, grew from microscopic

Discuss when and how members may or may not refer to scripture with others. List appropriate and inappropriate times.

CONNECTING WITH THE THEME

Invite participants to name the various theories they have heard about the beginning of the universe.

ABC's of the Bible

simple forms to more and more complex and specialized beings.

The book of Genesis explains things differently, because it comes from a society that was much less interested in science than we are. They were trying to explain the world they saw around them. They explained that everything was originally shapeless, and then things were made in stages. The sky with patterns of day and night, water below, and dry land full of growing vegetation were the first three stages, followed by the sun and moon that lived in the sky, the creatures that lived in the water, and the creatures that lived on the dry land.

Despite the differences, the Genesis story fits remarkably well with how we now explain things: The cosmos and the planets came first, then the live creatures to populate it. Seeing the similarities between the Genesis story and the modern stories of origin—or ignoring the likenesses in order to concentrate on differences so that we can decide that one version is right and the other is wrong—misses the point of Genesis. The Bible is not really interested in explaining what happened in prehistoric times. The Bible seeks to understand God. In other words, we should read the Bible not for the *how*, but *why*.

When we ask why, some answers appear. Why are things the way they are? Because God made them. Does it make sense? Yes, God made things in an orderly fashion. Are things always supposed to be just the way God made them? No, God makes things that multiply, fill the earth, grow, and change. What does God think of the world? God looked at the world and called it good. These are the enduring lessons of Genesis.

In the first chapter of the Gospel of John, the writer tells about Jesus in much the same way the writer of Genesis started out. All the other Gospels started out trying to answer the question about how

Discuss: How do the biblical and scientific explanations of the world help you or not help you understand the world and your role in it?

Read John 1:1–5.

Jesus got started. Matthew gives a genealogy and a story of Jesus' birth. Mark goes directly to Jesus' baptism. Luke tells more Christmas stories and even includes a story of Jesus as a young teen. John takes things further and says that the Word was with God from the beginning, and this Word entered into human flesh to become Jesus.

The Gospel writers did not attempt to report facts, but offered interpretations. They theologized—they told about who God is and what God was doing in the world at a deeper level. For Matthew, it was important that Jesus was always part of God's plan, a continuous development that fit in with all world history, especially with Israelite history. Mark jumped directly to what he considered most important: God's public announcement that Jesus is God's son, and the moment where Jesus took on a public ministry. These aren't contradictions; they both point to essential truths about God's work—God is always at work, and sometimes we need to focus on specific ways in which God does that work.

In Genesis, at the start of the gospels, and in many other places, the Bible theologizes. It tells us about God in sweeping terms. In a few sentences, it speaks volumes about who God is. God is always there, always acting, even before anything was created, or any part of the world we know came into being. God is not distant or aloof; each bird, each blade of grass, each human hair was made with care and deliberateness. That's who God is.

4. Encounter Jesus' tears 🔑

"Jesus began to weep." (John 11:35)

This is one of the shortest verses in the Bible. In some older translations the whole verse is "Jesus wept." Its brevity has been the reason that generations of youngsters have chosen this verse as something to memorize.

How does the beginning of John help you relate to God?

There's something about a two-word (or four-word) verse of scripture that seems almost silly. Most of scripture is in much longer sentences and verses. This one seems out of place. Furthermore, the sentence itself is on the verge of being too simplistic. If you believe crying is something almost everyone does, that it's normal and natural, then to say, "Jesus wept" is just stating the obvious. If you believe crying is something inappropriate in public, then "Jesus wept" seems embarrassing or scandalous.

Such a short and simple verse points out the uneven and arbitrary nature of versification in scripture. There is no reason why some verses are short and others long. The verse and chapter numbers are not reliable guides to what parts of the Bible belong together. In some cases they are actually misleading and can give the wrong impression if you take a single verse out of context, or if you read to the end of a chapter and miss the first few verses of the next one. There's no sure way to know how long a passage you need to read in order to come to a good stopping point. Counting the verses, or reading a whole chapter at a time, or similar strategies won't work all the time. Instead, you have to read for a while and make your own decisions.

Use a concordance to look up the name Lazarus. What other stories do you find about him? How do they broaden the picture and your understanding?

It may be obvious that we need to read more than "Jesus began to weep" in order to get the whole story. But how much further do we have to go? If we read John 11:31–35, we discover that Jesus and his friend Mary are talking, and they are sad that Lazarus, Mary's brother, has died. If we step back and get a bigger picture, we can see in verses 1–44 the story of how Jesus went to Lazarus with the intention of bringing him back from the dead.

Like creation stories, miracle stories point to the power of God at work in human life. A story of resurrection is an amazing demonstration of power, but it is more than power. The miracles reported in the gospels are not just arbitrary acts whereby Jesus counteracts the laws of nature to prove he has a special connection to God. That's not what miracles are about. Instead, miracles are ways of showing forth God's values, not just God's power. Life is a powerful value for God, and the desire to see people live full and meaningful lives motivates God and Jesus to great lengths, and even to miracles and other mighty acts of power.

In the short verse about Jesus weeping, we gain enormous insight into who God is and how God works through Jesus in the world. The one crying here is none other than Jesus, the Son of God, the Word who was in the beginning with God, who was God, and through whom all things were made, according to the first verses of the Gospel of John. This is God crying at the death of a beloved friend. God is moved to emotion from the depths of love. In this way, God is very much like us. It may be hard to imagine that God in the clouds of heaven weeps uncontrollably at some human death. But we worship a God who is emotionally involved, who cries at a friend's death, who holds the hurting alongside the tomb and sobs with them. From this short verse in John, we feel reassured that God holds us and cries with us in our moments of pain.

Name and list images members have heard about God, such as mighty fortress, mother hen, or eagle. Look up *God* or *Names of God* in a Bible dictionary to compare to the group's list.

5. Seek God's wisdom 🗝

"*K*eep straight the path of your feet, and all your ways will be sure." (Proverbs 4:26)

The book of Proverbs is a classic example of ancient Israel's wisdom. If you have a Bible with the Apocrypha (books written between the time of the Old and New Testaments, often appearing in Bibles between the two Testaments), you have other books of wisdom: the book of Sirach (also called Ben Sira) and the Wisdom of Solomon. These books contain advice for daily living, arranged in short sentences.

ABC's of the Bible

They cover personal relationships, parenting, virtues such as truth and charity, proper business conduct, avoiding dangers and temptations, dealing with government officials, and so forth. Some of them are common sense, and many of them contain deep insight into the human character.

The proverbs often seem strange, because they come from a different culture. Verses about kings or scales in the marketplace are true today, although we have to adjust to the parallel situations in our experience. Proverbs 22:13 says: "The lazy person says, 'There is a lion outside! I shall be killed in the streets!' " Probably none of us have heard someone say this phrase, since not many lions run loose where we live. We may know, however, people who make up excuses for laziness. We also need to be careful to remember that this wisdom comes from a society where adult men experienced more privilege than was probably good for anyone. Some people have read verses like Proverbs 13:24 and 22:15, which talk about using rods or heavy sticks to beat children into obedience, and in so doing committed horrible acts of abuse. We must resist the misinterpretations of scripture that can create the abuse of women and children.

If we use caution in our reading and interpretation, we can gain a great deal of wisdom from these ancient proverbs. Many of them communicate values we need to hear today. Honesty, trustworthiness, loyalty, and hard work provide good values now. Morality is an important part of God's work with us and our life with God, and scripture provides wonderful resources in Proverbs and other wisdom books (as well as other parts of the Bible) for discerning how to act rightly.

Proverbs offers a needed balance to other parts of the Bible, to show us the full range of God's vision for humanity. God is creator and miracle-worker, but we must not think that God is active only in those

Quickly skim other verses in Proverbs. What helpful or unhelpful sayings do you notice?

bigger-than-life moments. God is concerned with our actions every day, and the Bible gives us a moral vision that can help us each day of our lives.

6. Think of others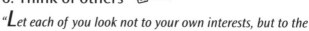

"Let each of you look not to your own interests, but to the interests of others." (Philippians 2:4)

CONNECTING WITH LIFE

Philippians is another letter Paul wrote to one of the early Christian churches, this one located in the city of Philippi. Paul thinks in great theological terms, in the best tradition of scripture that seeks to understand the nature and purpose of God and to give these insights the fullest expression. But Paul does not speak to the church only in the abstract; he has in mind specific people whom he knows by name. This keeps him focused. In this letter, he talks of the humility of Christ and for the need for people to keep their own egos in check so that they can cooperate with one another. Twice he encourages the Philippians to be blameless (1:10 and 2:15; Paul portrays himself as blameless in 3:6). This is the context for 2:4: think about one another, not just about yourself. Don't let yourself sink into petty squabbling over who deserves the most and who should get the most in the church or in life. Think instead about Jesus' example as a humble person.

Paul had in mind a specific conflict within the local church in Philippi, although we cannot be certain exactly what it was. He names specific situations where there is strife (especially in 4:2), but he may have had in mind something larger within the Christian community. Paul's words in this book of scripture have a more far-reaching implication. We can see power struggles today within institutions, churches, and other religious groups. Clearly, Paul would want us to avoid that kind of strife. The disagreements between churches that can drain the strength of the Christian witness would probably also be disturbing to him.

Discuss: How can we take Paul's words further, to include the ways our society divides itself into the have and have-nots? If we each look to other's interests, what will we do about poverty, unemployment, homelessness, racism, sexism, and other problems of our culture?

Right after Paul tells the Philippians to think of one another first, he recites a poem or hymn that was probably familiar to the Philippians and other early Christians (2:6–11). Once we start thinking of others, it seems natural for praise to follow, because we praise God made known to us in Christ as the center of our lives, from which all the rest of our daily lives follow. This hymn of praise to Christ ends with the vision of the entire world confessing that Jesus is the Christ to the glory of God. With this grand vision of the whole world in mind, we would be mistaken to think that Paul's advice pertains only to the squabbles within the church. Paul advocates humility, blamelessness, and concern for others not just to help the church, but to bring the whole world to a recognition of God's good news.

7. Claim images of God

The beginning of Genesis paints a picture of a creative God involved in fashioning the universe, from the large cosmos to individual people. Modern astronomy helps us see the vastness of the universe as we build larger telescopes that help us see farther into the universe. A few words in the Gospel of John point to a compassionate God who cries and suffers with the hurts of the world. Which image helps you relate to God? Which helps you understand God in a new way? Which image do you find yourself relating to on a day-to-day basis? How does it feel to try to hold both images of God together?

Invite members to select the image they find most helpful. Does one image seem more popular than the other, or are they evenly balanced?

8. Magnify the Lord 🔑

"Mary said, 'My soul magnifies the Lord, and my spirit rejoices in God my Savior.'" (Luke 1:46–47)

One of the great hymns of the Bible comes from Mary, the mother of Jesus. When Mary knew she was pregnant, she spent three months with her relative Elizabeth, who was also pregnant. Elizabeth was an

CONNECTING WITH GOD

older woman who never expected to add to her family at that age; Mary was a young woman with an unexpected pregnancy before she was married. People all over must have talked about these two pregnant women, and some of what they said must have been awful and cruel. Together, Mary and Elizabeth found understanding and acceptance with each other. Encouraged by Elizabeth's love, Mary sang a song that begins, "My soul magnifies the Lord." Tradition has called the song the Magnificat; it praises God for not only choosing Mary as the mother of Jesus but also for God's work to set things right in the world and to show mercy to those who need it.

When people recognize God's hand at work in the world, praise results. God works in ways large and small all the time, through creation, miracles, common sense, and the love of people. Through reading the Bible, we can learn to recognize the signs of what God and God's people are doing, and then it is our turn to give praise, like Hannah, Mary, and so many others before us.

See how Mary's song in Luke 1:46–55 echoes Hannah's prayer in 1 Samuel 2:1–10.

How do you praise God individually? as a group? What type of praise feels comfortable? awkward? How can you open yourself to new forms of praise?

9. Pray together

Dear God,

We have seen you at work in creation,
we have read stories of your miracles,
we have learned how you cry with us in our hurts,
and we have felt the love of your people.

Teach us to praise you for all this.
Show us ways to be your people
in our daily lives.

Amen.

Pray together the unison prayer.

NOTES

4

Finding Faith and Hope

(N through Q)

Before the session, make a list of things where you have made positive changes in your life lately. Think about the areas where you need to work and pray to do what is right for others.

Session Focus: The Bible provides stories of faithful people who have struggled through difficult times. In the midst of struggle, they found hope in God. By hearing their stories, we can find hope for our lives and discover God's presence among us.

Focus Scriptures: Hebrews 11:1; Psalm 130:1; Ezekiel 37:4; Ecclesiastes 9:17

In the past sessions, several of the verses have concentrated on ethics. Much of the Bible focuses on what humans should do as part of their responsibility to God in faith. We have learned verses such as "Do to others as you would have them do to you" and "Let each of you look not to your own interests, but to the interests of others." How have these verses made a difference in your life? Have you had the opportunity to reflect on your own ethical practices?

Other verses have concentrated on praise. God has done much for us, from creation to Jesus to personal involvement in each day's joys and pains. When have

Make a list of God's praiseworthy actions you have seen or experienced.

Discuss the process of memorizing verses and their impact on group members.

Invite group members to name places where they feel close to God or activities that connect them to God.

Discuss: What does it feel like when you feel that God has abandoned you? When do you feel most empty and alone?

Invite participates to name resources that help connect them to God.

you seen God at work? When have you taken time to praise God for what you have seen, or asked God for clarity to see more of what God is doing in people's lives?

1. Review previous verses

Which verses from the past three sessions have impacted your life? How have they affected the way you view your faith and the world? Which verses have been easier to memorize? Which have carried the most meaning for you?

Discuss the questions listed in "Before the Session," which deal with how we live our faith and for what we praise God. While memorization can help us retain words for later recall, we need to also discuss the implications of the words to help the meaning impact our lives.

2. Recognize God's presence

Sometimes God feels very close to us. This happens for people in many different ways. Maybe you feel close to God when you are at church, alone reading scripture or praying, sharing a special moment with your family, or in beautiful places of nature. Think about where you are and what you are doing when God feels closest to you.

On the other hand, sometimes it's very difficult to sense God's presence. God may sometimes feel distant and unrelated to our lives. This can leave an emptiness or even a feeling of being abandoned by God. There's nothing unusual about these feelings; we all feel this way sometimes. Even Jesus prayed from the cross, "My God, my God, why have you forsaken me?" (Matthew 27:46, where Jesus quotes Psalm 22:1).

Spirituality has become very popular in recent years. Many books, resources, practices, and workshops exist to help us feel spiritual. When have you tried any of these? Which resources helped you feel more connected to God?

3. Define faith

*"**N**ow faith is the assurance of things hoped for, the conviction of things not seen."* (Hebrews 11:1)

The Gospel of Mark tells a fascinating story. When people heard that Jesus was home, the crowd started to swell. The house was full, and no one else could get near the door. Some people brought their friend who could not walk to meet Jesus. When they got to Jesus' house, there was no way to get Jesus' attention. The friends climbed onto the roof, cut a hole, and lowered their friend through the roof into the middle of the crowd. Jesus looked at the man, looked at his friends, and said to the man, "Because of their faith, your sins are forgiven." After some people argued over whether or not what Jesus did was right, Jesus healed the man's legs.

Sometimes, we make a connection between faith and salvation. We think we need to have the right kind of faith in order to be saved. But this isn't the right way to think about faith. Faith is not something we possess in order to make God like us. Faith is God's gift to people. It is not something we do to earn God's favor.

Faith does have effects. Our faith is best used when it is a belief in the good news that God is saving the world. It becomes motivation for us to show care for the world to join God in the world's redemption and salvation.

In the words of Hebrews, faith is the assurance of what we do not yet see. Through faith, we know God loves the world and has been at work through Jesus and through us to save the world. But the reality is that we look at the world and have a hard time recognizing if God is having any effect on the world. When we read the newspaper, when we talk with

Read Mark 2:1–5.

Create a list of other words or phrases that come to mind when you hear the word *faith*. Read other passages about faith: Ephesians 2:8–9; Romans 1:11–12. How do these passages relate to your list of words and phrases?

our friends, or when we look at our lives, it is easy to become depressed and lose heart. We can see that things are not the way God wants them to be. We do not see a world we think God would love, and we do not see a world God is in the midst of saving.

Faith reminds us that God is gracious and merciful, constantly saving the unlovely, and finding ways to work for good in a world that seems intent on the opposite. Faith reminds us of the things that have gone right in this world. Evidence may be hard to see in the rough times, but God is still at work, and faith is God's gift to offer us the certainty and conviction that God's loving activity is not limited to what we see.

4. Face difficult times

"Out of the depths I cry to you, O Lord." (Psalm 130:1)

Even people of faith will encounter difficult times when hope seems far away. When disaster, disease, divorce, death, or other distress strikes us, there seems little to do but cry. In these times, faith can help. Faith teaches us what we cannot see and gives us hope, for it reveals to us that God works even while events seem irredeemable. Perhaps it is at these times that God cries with us as well.

When have you felt in the depths of despair? When have you cried out to God?

When difficulties hit, we may wonder whether we deserve the bad things that happen. Often we cry out that these horrible things aren't fair, that we do not deserve them, that we should not be forced to suffer like we do. But at another level comes the nagging fear that we may well have earned what is happening. After all, we are sinners. We have failed God, and we have denied and betrayed God's purposes in the world. We have sinned, and the Bible assesses that the wages of sin are death (Romans 6:23). In times of deepest despair, faith is what enables us to think that God will not count our sins against us.

Whatever we deserve will not strike at us. The evils we have perpetrated on the world will not be

perpetrated on us in any attempt to even the score. God will not try to solve evil with evil, even if all the rest of us try that strategy.

In the language of this psalm, we wait on God for redemption. Faith is the recognition that only God can deal with the problems of the world, that our attempts are not adequate by themselves. We need God, and God will act. The problems of the day are temporary; God will redeem. Faith holds together the tension between God's saving vision and the realities of the present world.

5. Hear prophecy

"Prophesy to these bones, and say to them: O dry bones, hear the word of the LORD. Thus says the Lord GOD to these bones: I will cause breath to enter you, and you shall live." (Ezekiel 37:4)

In modern times, prophecy is usually thought of as foreseeing the future or as telling what will happen. When you go through the grocery store checkout line, you see the tabloids with horoscopes and predictions. The Bible's prophets are completely different from these images. In the Bible, prophecy is not about seeing into the future; it's about seeing the present with greater clarity, more depth, and keen insight. It's the art or talent of understanding what's really going on, instead of just what's in the headlines or being talked about among neighbors.

Prophecy understands that God is at work in the world and is an active participant in what happens. Although world events and local happenings often seem disconnected from God's will, in God's perspective all things eventually will be transformed into the world that God desires. Prophecy isn't about telling the future; it's about telling the truth in a world so obsessed with the moment that it fails to see the deeper reality of God's work.

Ezekiel prophesied during the exile, a time when Israel was suffering military defeat and the leaders of

Read Psalm 130.

What images come to mind when you hear the word prophet?

Who are the prophets in today's world? How do they relate to the biblical role of prophets?

Find the longer books of prophecy (Isaiah, Jeremiah, and Ezekiel) and the twelve shorter books (Hosea through Malachi).

When have you felt as though you were standing in a valley of dry bones? What helped bring the bones to life?

Israel were taken from their land to Babylonia. Many people saw these events as the death of the nation and their way of life. They focused on their losses; Ezekiel redirected their attention to God's action in the world.

Ezekiel sees things as if in a vision. God takes him to a dry, deserted valley. Ezekiel looks around him, and all he sees are dry bones—evidence of a former battle that Israel has lost horrendously.

God asks the prophet, "Can these bones live?" On the surface, the answer is no. Dead bones don't live. In the world we know, resurrection doesn't occur. But Ezekiel knows that what he sees and what God sees are not always the same. Ezekiel cannot see any hope, but maybe God can. So Ezekiel answers, "Only you know, O God."

God tells Ezekiel to prophesy to the bones and to tell them the truth—God will send the spirit to live in the bones once more, and the bones will rise and live. As Ezekiel speaks these words to the bones, the Spirit rushes in like a wind through the valley of death. The wind shakes the bones, they start to rattle, and soon they begin to move. The bones begin to strike each other and stick together, and soon they stick together until they look like skeletons. Sinews grow onto these newly animated skeletons, muscles and tendons take shape, and flesh grows over them. Soon the people are rebuilt, brought back to life through the wind of God's Spirit.

We see death in the world around us. God sees something more. God sees the potential for new life, powered by God's Spirit, as what it takes to change the world and bring good news of new life in God to the ends of the earth. Prophecy helps us connect what we do not see with what God sees.

CONNECTING WITH LIFE

6. Hear the quiet words

"Quiet words of the wise are more to be heeded than the shouting of a ruler among fools." (Ecclesiastes 9:17)

Prophecy tries to discern God's action in the midst of everyday life with all its problems, joys, and daily events. When we begin to lose hope because we cannot see God's presence, prophecy reminds us that God remains at work in the world. But at the same time, prophecy can sometimes have an unintended side effect: It can encourage us to ignore what's around us in favor of things that have not yet come to pass. For this reason, prophecy must be balanced with other witnesses from scripture. Prophecy by itself provides only a faith in what has not yet been seen; as people who are God's partners, we must also concentrate on the here and now.

Changing the world is a huge task. We do not complete it by ourselves. There is no fast, easy solution to the world's problems, which is precisely why the world needs God's love and salvation. Prophecy tells us that God will bring God's reign to the world and that change will happen. We can make a difference, because we are God's partners in announcing the good news. But this does not mean that everything we do will have visible, positive, instant results.

Ecclesiastes is a book like Proverbs, in that they are both wisdom books. Proverbs, however, is much more concerned with advice about how to live moral lives, whereas Ecclesiastes is a more contemplative book, wondering about how things really work. Ecclesiastes concludes that much of what we do does not make the difference we wish it would. We are not in control of our circumstances or of what affects us.

Read Ecclesiastes 3:16–22; 9:11–12.

Ecclesiastes knows that disaster strikes good and bad people alike, and that there are real limits to how much we can change in our lives. Death comes to all in the end, and Ecclesiastes finds that we can never be certain about what comes after life. There is only faith, and faith is the assurance of what we do not see.

Many people find Ecclesiastes depressing. This book tells us that much of what we do will not make

When have you felt that something you did made no difference at all?

any difference at all, nor will it be remembered after we are gone. But there is also a strong hope in these words. Our faith is misplaced if it is in what we can do, just as our faith is misplaced if we count on God to do everything and take no responsibility ourselves. In between these extremes is the right kind of faith, for it gives us hope in God's activity and empowers us to join with God without thinking we are in control of the world. When prophecy shifts our attention away from everyday life, Ecclesiastes reminds us we have limits; we are not responsible for making sure God's plan happens right now. We have work, but we have opportunities to enjoy daily life, as well. The thousand small joys of everyday living can and should be ours. There is no reason to forget about the mundane essence of life or to forsake its joys for a larger purpose. The larger purpose is God's, and we join it for a time but we do not take it over. It would be foolish to take over God's place. We should listen to the quiet words of the wise, do our part, and leave the rest to God. Finding this middle ground of faith is not easy, but it is wise.

What joys of everyday living do you enjoy? How do you find God in the mundane tasks of life?

7. Find a center in life

How do we find a center to life? How do we navigate between the extremes? Scripture provides us with a multitude of responses to these questions. Sometimes, different parts of the Bible have different emphases that push us in different directions. Together these scriptures can provide a balance for our living.

God is ever near us. Our work with God does make a difference, but we should not think that everything in our life is work. God does not love us on the basis of the work we do to bring God's reign closer to the world. God does not love us or save us because of what we do. God loves us and invites us to join in meaningful work in the world, but God also wants us to enjoy living in the world at hand.

When has your work for God become a task rather than a joy? What do you do when you no longer enjoy the work you do for God? How does the church respond to people who need to take a break from church work?

Because God's love comes first, our relationship with God is of crucial importance. We need to stay close to God, and that's more important than the tasks we tackle on God's behalf.

CONNECTING WITH GOD

Discuss how group members can help one another try new ways to experience God's presence.

8. Experience God's presence

How do you feel God's presence in your life? Mark the following things that help you experience God's presence:

____ praying with others

____ praying alone

____ daily scripture readings

____ worship

____ meditations about life and faith

____ experiences of Christian community

____ talking things through with friends

____ helping others in service

____ singing

____ playing an instrument

____ planning and implementing a church event

____ other _____

How can you improve your sense of God's presence in your life this week? What new things would you like to try to experience God's presence?

Divide into two groups. Ask each group to prayerfully read the following parts.

9. Pray together

1 and 2:	Our God,
1:	*we thank you for being with us*
2:	*through faith, through worship,*
1:	*through challenging words, through quiet words.*
1 and 2:	*We ask that you be in our hearts*
1:	*in assuring ways seen and unseen,*
2:	*in the very depths of our souls,*
1:	*like life in our bones,*
2:	*like wise words on our tongues.*
1:	*Keep us close to you*
2:	*in this week and always.*
1 and 2:	*Amen.*

NOTES

5

Embracing God and One Another

(R through V)

Session Focus: Through love, God provided instructions to help us live lives of fullness. In response to this love, God calls us to love God and one another.

Focus Scriptures: Exodus 20:8; Isaiah 55:6; 61:1; Psalm 127:1; Luke 3:4

BEFORE THE SESSION

See Romans 12:5 and 1 Corinthians 12:2.

Faith in God has both inner and outer aspects, and neither can be neglected. In the previous session we concentrated on images of the inner life and on the sense of God's presence with us. We sometimes downplay the ways faith gets acted out and may only emphasize that God lives in our hearts, but God is present in the world in many ways. The feeling of connection to God we receive through prayer and other spiritual practices is only part of the picture. *God* is also present in the world through *our* actions. Because of what we do, others can feel God's presence.

Paul writes about Christians as the body of Christ. We are Christ's body in the world now. We are connected together, and one part of the body affects all the members. If God's presence through Christ is to be seen and touched and felt and believed in the world today, it is through Christ's body—through us. We are God's hands and feet and heart and mouth in the world today, and we are God's primary way for making God's presence known in the world.

That is why ethics are so important for the Christian life. What we do with our lives and how we make everyday choices has enormous consequence because we are Christ's body at work in the world. We are the incarnation of God for our time. The world looks at us in order to see God.

1. Recall God's presence

Think about your daily activities during the past week. When did you sense God's presence this week? through other people? through activities? as you struggled during a crisis? as you joyfully celebrated?

How might others have come closer to God because of what you did during the past week? How might your decisions and actions have served the body of Christ? How do you make ethical decisions? What biblical laws help you make decisions?

2. Remember the Sabbath

"Remember the sabbath day, and keep it holy." (Exodus 20:8)

When God decided to rescue the people of Israel from Egypt, where they were slaves, God brought them out of the land through the leadership of Moses. The Egyptians had oppressed the Israelites with political sanctions, economic punishments, and military threats, and they faced other difficulties once they left Egypt. While the Israelites wandered for forty years in the desert, they worried about finding their next meal. At times they thought they would not have enough water to drink and would die from thirst and dehydration.

Almost none of the original Israelites survived the forty years in the wilderness before reaching the land God promised them. Although most did die in the desert, they lived on as a people, and over the centuries they began to regard this ancient experience as a source of renewal and new beginnings. With the benefit of hindsight, they could see that change could not happen in a single generation, but being God's people and changing their way of life was the best thing for them.

In the desert, God gave the Israelites many gifts. Freedom from Egyptian slavery was only the first gift. God gave them food to eat and water to drink. God gave them leadership, in the form of Moses and a pillar of cloud by day and fire by night to guide them. But they remembered one thing as God's greatest gift: the law.

Christians have a difficult time relating to the idea of law. As people of faith, many of our traditions think of law as the opposite of grace, and the New Testament proclaims that we are saved by grace, not by the things we do in adherence to the law. Truly, salvation and life with God is not something to be earned, but it is something that changes our lives and redirects our actions, just as any relationship changes us and encourages us to perform acts of love and kindness.

Law is not only a religious problem for Christians today; it's also a cultural problem. We associate the law with a complicated set of rules and regulations that can feel arbitrary and limiting. The law says we can drive at fifty-five miles per hour, but not at fifty-six miles per hour. Why draw the line there? The law says that for every dollar I spend at the store, I have to give the state and local government a half-dozen cents—and I do not have any direct say about how much I'll give in taxes or what it will be spent on. We don't like the law because it takes away our right to choose how fast to drive, what to spend our

What feelings do you experience when you hear the word *law*?

What laws do you
face each day? How
do you feel
about them?

money on, and a thousand other things in daily life.
In our culture, we resent that immensely. So the idea
of God's law has problems in our culture.

But the ancient Israelites saw things very differently
than we do. They saw the law of God as a gift, something God gave them in the desert. It was a perfect
gift—it was just what they needed. The law was a set of
instructions for their lives. It made sense out of life and
gave their actions meaning, purpose, and organization. It
would be better if we would not translate the Hebrew
word *Torah* as "law," but as "instruction." In most cases,
it's easier to build something if you pay attention to the
instructions, and the result is better and stronger. In the
same way, life is usually better if you live according to
God's instructions.

The Sabbath law as part of the Ten Commandments
was a vital part of these instructions. For this twenty-
four hour period each week, the people of God were
different. They were different from the other people of
the world, from the followers of other gods, and from
the way they were the rest of the week. Instead of
working and doing the everyday tasks, these faithful
people concentrated on their faith and their relationship with God. The Sabbath was a time of prayer and
concentration, a time to become focused on the most
important part of their lives. The rest of life is important, but one day a week is right to give fully to the
relationship with God and to concentrate on why we
live instead of how to live or make a living.

Read Exodus
20:9–11.

3. Experience holiness

*"Seek the LORD while he may be found, call upon him while he
is near."* (Isaiah 55:6)

The law gives a way for people of faith to be different
than others. The Ten Commandments and other parts of
the Bible call this difference *holiness* or *consecration,* words
meaning "set apart." God is separate or different from
us, and so we should be separate from the rest of the

See Exodus 19.

What words or images come to mind when you hear the word *holiness*?

Name ways you keep the Sabbath. How do these ways help you reconnect to God?

world, instead of becoming like it. Holiness is a means of resistance against the world's ways of doing things, in order to be more like God.

The story of how Israel received the law—the instructions of Torah—emphasizes the holiness of separation. When the people were wandering in the wilderness, they came close to a mountain in the desert. God told Moses they could speak together at the top of that mountain. God gave the people three days to get ready, and they washed to be clean for God's appearance. But washing and cleanliness wasn't enough. God told Moses to set limits around the mountain. No one would be allowed to come within those limits when God was on the mountain. The degree of separation was so great that the people had to keep their distance from God. The Torah was the way in which God would bridge the gap between them.

Holiness requires this kind of separation. Holiness means the recognition that God and people are different and that it takes God's loving, powerful action to bridge the gulf of difference. For this reason, Israel must keep the Sabbath and perform all the other laws to be like God rather than the other people of the world. To be like God is to be different than others, but also to struggle to bridge the differences between people. Holiness recognizes the differences, refuses to ignore them, and lives in the midst of great difference in order to bridge the gaps between people and between people and God.

This complex idea of holiness or separation works throughout the Old and New Testaments. Because it is such a complex idea, it is hard to understand all at once. Often the Bible emphasizes one part of it at a time to make it easier. A lot of the law and the priestly regulations emphasize that Israel should be separate from the other nations. Cleanliness, dedication, ritual, and other things are part of maintaining holiness. It reminds everyone of the distance and the difference.

But we worship a God who bridges the distance, and many of the prophets emphasize this part of holiness. Because God is deeply concerned about us, God is interested in what we do every day—not just on Sabbaths. Isaiah reminds us to seek God while God can be found, for God is near to us. This is no distant God, but one who breaks the barriers between us. This God reaches out to touch us, and yet we need to respond. Touching God—and letting God touch us—is never easy. We should never take for granted the privilege of finding God.

How do you separate yourself from the world?

This is why the law, ethics, and faithful action are all so important to the life of faith. The Torah provides instructions about how to be closer to God. The Torah teaches holiness, the means of being different from the world in order to be like God. We need that instruction, for without it we would stumble even more often in our attempts to live life close to God. God reaches out to us in many ways, including the instruction of the law, but it still takes our response to God's reaching. In Paul's terms, we are the body of Christ, and we must reach out to embrace God, just as we are God's embrace of the world.

4. Reach out to others

"The spirit of the Lord God is upon me, because the Lord has anointed me." (Isaiah 61:1)

God's Spirit reaches out to touch us in our daily lives, giving us not only the sense of God's presence but the motivation to action that makes us part of God's people and God's body in the world today. When God's Spirit is with us, then we act as partners with God.

Read Isaiah 61:1–4.

In ancient Israel, the prophet Isaiah announced that God's Spirit had arrived; God had anointed the prophet to do God's work. The partnership of God and humanity was embodied in this one person, but not just in this one person. The Spirit is not a special possession of a single individual or of a select few. It is not a privilege for only the special ones, nor a gift given only to God's chosen ones. The Spirit is poured out upon all God's people as a way of living life in God's presence and as God's partners.

God's Spirit brings us the task, the power, the presence, and the partnership to be God's agents in the world to care for hurting and disadvantaged people and to comfort the sad and distressed. When we do the work of God in the world, then we display God's glory to a world distant from God. The world may not see God, for they have not listened to the law and they have not learned how to seek God. But when we are filled with the Spirit, we do these things to display God's glory to the world.

When Jesus began his ministry as God's partner on earth, he referred to these words of Isaiah 61. This ancient work of God was Jesus' ministry. Jesus proclaimed that the scripture was fulfilled on that day in the hearing of those who worshiped God with him in the synagogue.

Scripture needs to be fulfilled repeatedly. God keeps reaching out to the world. What Jesus does is to live his life in accord with scripture. He follows the instructions of God, the same instructions that come down to us through the Torah. *Fulfilling* the scriptures doesn't mean it's over. Instead, maybe we should say that the scriptures *filled* Jesus. Jesus lived his life fully dedicated to this kind of ministry. Neither Isaiah nor Jesus was the last word in God's reaching out to the world, because God keeps reaching. Today, God reaches through us when we do the same things that the prophet and Jesus did, as members of the body of Christ.

How can we do these things to which God calls us? How can we become like God and help a hurting world? What do we do to display God's glory?

Compare Isaiah's words in Isaiah 61:1–4 to what Jesus said in Luke 4:14–21. What did Jesus imply by reading these words from Isaiah?

How do you reach out to others as part of the body of Christ?

ABC's of the Bible

5. Rely on God 🔑

"Unless the LORD builds the house, those who build it labor in vain. Unless the LORD guards the city, the guard keeps watch in vain." (Psalm 127:1)

From this psalm comes an important reminder: It is not our activity that achieves the goal, but God is the one who builds the house of faith, guards the cities in which we all live, and saves the world. Although we are called to be God's partners, we are completely dependent upon God.

The purpose of working as the body of Christ and following the instructions of the Torah is to live life with God and to bring the world and God closer together. We must rely on God. Our partnership with God means we can not do it on our own. The instructions of the law remind us of the differences between God and us. We are not God—we are God's partners. We do not set the agenda for what God is doing in the world. The business of the church is set neither by our boards and committees nor by church growth consultants and denominational agencies. God provides the mission of the church for God's purposes—to love and save the world. All our other work will fail. Only when we rely on God and join God's plans will we succeed.

The church has founded many monastic orders, and many other faithful Christians have lived lives of self-denial. Others choose to rely on God for healing instead of accepting the health advantages of modern medicine; some expect God to provide them with money for living. All these can serve as powerful expressions of faith. But the matter of reliance on God is most directly concerned with getting the house built and the city guarded, in the words of the psalmist—or in our words, reliance on God is a matter of accepting God's priorities for the world.

We cannot bridge the gap between God and us on our terms. We cannot convince God to live life

How do you discern God's plans? What plans has your congregation made? How do they fit with God's plans? What is your congregation's mission? How does it match God's purposes?

What would your life look like if you relied solely on God?

What changes have you made in your path? How do you follow the direction of God's activity in the world?

Read Luke 3:3–6 and compare to Isaiah 40:1–5.

according to our plans and to serve our wants and desires. But God keeps persuading us to join God and to rely on God.

6. Follow God's path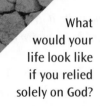

"The Voice of one crying out in the wilderness: 'Prepare the way of the Lord, make his paths straight.'" (Luke 3:4)

John the Baptist traveled throughout the countryside telling people to prepare for the coming of God's anointed one, the Christ, whom John recognized as his cousin, Jesus. John preached that the people needed repentance, a changing of their path in life so they were in accord with the instructions of the Torah and the direction of God's activity in the world. John understood that people's actions were important, because it was through the activity of people and the work of God that the vision of God's rule would become reality.

Luke's image of John's preaching comes from the prophet Isaiah. Isaiah spoke of a time when a group of worshipers of God would move from Babylon, where they were servants of a foreign emperor, back to Jerusalem, where they could dedicate themselves afresh to the service of God. When these people returned to Jerusalem, then God's presence would be in this city once more. Isaiah envisions that even nature would join as partner in making this happen—the curvy roads would straighten out and the ups and downs of the road would level out so God's people would have an easy path.

The goal is, in Isaiah's words, "the glory of the Lord shall be revealed, and all people shall see it together," or in the interpretation of Luke's words, "all flesh shall see the salvation of God." Such is the goal that called John, called Jesus, and calls Jesus' followers today. The goal is to help the world see God and God's desires for the world.

But as much as Isaiah, John, and millions of followers afterward have wished for an easy path, it has never been that way. It was hard to follow God in ancient Jerusalem when other world empires controlled the world. John the Baptist certainly had a difficult life: existing in poverty, living in the wilderness with a message that made him very unpopular with the religious leaders, and eventually being imprisoned and executed for his outspokenness on God's behalf. These people insisted on ethical action in a world that resisted the idea of right action. There was no easy path.

For us today, the path of God is not easy either. We may wish for convenient transportation on our journey with God, but the reality is that the road is tough. Jesus described it as a narrow path: "Enter through the narrow gate; for the gate is wide and the road is easy that leads to destruction, and there are many who take it. For the gate is narrow and the road is hard that leads to life, and there are few who find it" (Matthew 7:13–14). What God asks of us is not easy, but it is the path of life.

When have you encountered a difficult path but wished for an easier road to follow? What helped you continue along the journey?

CONNECTING WITH GOD

Reflect on the ethical issues of the day.

List how members help God embrace the world. What similarities and differences do you notice?

7. Embrace God and the world

What are key issues for the church's attention? What should Christians do about these issues? Do not think only about the issues that get a lot of attention in the newspapers and television. What are the issues you face every day? Where are there people hurting? How is the world different from the world God would want?

What can we do to make a difference, to make the world more like God's desire? How can we embrace the world so they can sense God's presence and touch through us? What is most difficult in all of this for you? Where do you need the most help?

While some may find the preceding questions stimulating and challenging, others may find them overwhelming. We do not all help God embrace the world in the same way. For some, active participation in building a house with Habitat for Humanity for a family may show God's presence. Others may express God's care through deep prayer for people who are hurting. Recognize that we need a variety of ways to help God embrace the world.

8. Pray together

Our God, you lead us through difficult paths.

Please keep our steps direct
and keep our eyes focused on you.

We want to travel your road
and to walk this journey with you.

We have caught your vision;
we have joined your body;
we choose to live as your partners.

Thank you for the instruction of the law,
and for the power of holiness in the world.

Thank you for the ways you come close to us,
and let us reach out to touch you.

Empower us to do what is right,
to make your world see your glory
in all that we do.

Amen.

Select a leader to read the regular type, and invite others to read responsively the bold type.

NOTES

6

Continuing the Scripture Journey

(W through Z)

Session Focus: God calls us to follow God's path of kindness and justice. As we read God's instructions and examine our love for Christ, we will respond in love to God and one another.

Focus Scriptures: Micah 6:8; 2 Corinthians 13:5; Psalm 119:105; Luke 19:5

BEFORE THE SESSION

Before meeting for this last session, review the last five sessions.

Look again at the key verses you have studied during the past five sessions. What verses have stayed in your mind? Which verses have made a difference in what you do throughout the week?

Think about the major themes you discussed together. How would you summarize to a friend the two or three most important things you have learned about the Bible?

We make commitments to people or activities we feel are important. While we may feel reading the Bible is a good idea, we may find the practice of regular reading a difficult challenge. As we read, we encounter a culture different from our own, and we discover names and places that seem unfamiliar. Some rules and views of the world seem foreign, and we may get easily discouraged. "I just don't understand what I'm reading" is a common statement among those who give up the practice of reading the Bible.

As mentioned earlier in this series, commentaries, dictionaries, and other resources can help one understand the context and background of the Bible. An encounter with the Bible may come more alive, however, in the context of a small group of people struggling to understand its meaning in relation to their lives. Study with a small group or find a few friends to join you in the process. Whichever method you choose, invite God to speak to you as you listen to God call you from the words upon the page.

CONNECTING WITH ONE ANOTHER

As the session begins, tell one another favorite verses from previous sessions.

1. Recall Bible verses

During the past five sessions, you have encountered twenty-two Bible verses from A through V. This final session concludes with verses W to Z. What verses have impacted your life during the past weeks? What major themes have been important to you?

If you chose to memorize the verses, which ones have been easy to learn? Which have been difficult? How has the discipline of memorization affected other areas of your life?

As a group, describe what was at the heart of Jesus' message. Describe what it might have been like to be one of the early Christians. What difference do you feel in your personal faith or in your commitment to living out the gospel?

CONNECTING WITH THE THEME

2. Discern what God requires 🔑

"What does the LORD require of you but to do justice, and to love kindness, and to walk humbly with your God?" (Micah 6:8)

Continuing the Scripture Journey

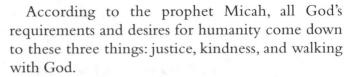

According to the prophet Micah, all God's requirements and desires for humanity come down to these three things: justice, kindness, and walking with God.

Justice is an important word throughout the Old Testament. In our world, we typically talk of a justice system, by which we mean laws, police, courts, and prisons. Justice in our culture is a way to right the wrongs, but it usually works by punishing those who have broken the law and have been caught. In the Bible, however, justice refers to life the way it should be lived. Justice is what happens when people live according to the instructions of the Torah for daily living. People share community with one another in right relationships. We care for each other and do whatever it takes to show compassion toward one another. We refuse all the ways we could take advantage of others or victimize others for personal gain. We think instead of God's whole people and the created world at large, and we work for the good of all.

Justice in the Bible is much more than retribution and punishment. Even when things are horribly broken, justice means restoration. It means healing and rebuilding. In the prophetic vision examined in the previous session, Isaiah spoke of rebuilding the cities that had been destroyed. This would be an act of justice. In today's inner cities and urban areas, justice is not about building more prisons and locking up the criminals. It is not about lowering the crime rate. Justice is about rebuilding. Justice creates new worlds in the midst of the old. Justice holds forth new ways of life that are rich and full and meaningful, because these ways of life are tightly connected to God's interwoven community of people. In just communities, people care for one another out of love. This is what Micah means when he says God wants us to do justice.

Loving-kindness takes even a further step. "Kindness" is a translation of the Hebrew word

What other verses in this study or elsewhere in the Bible help you understand the justice God requires of us?

ABC's of the Bible

Look up how this word is translated in different Bible versions.

hesed. It's a difficult word to translate. Hesed is sometimes translated as loyalty or faithfulness. If justice is about creating a world where everyone can live safe, healthy, full lives, hesed is about making that world even better by going the second mile for those whom we love. A kind or loyal relationship, a relationship with hesed, occurs when my life is so connected to yours that I willingly, eagerly do something extra for you. It is not because you deserve it or because I'll get something in return, but because our lives are so intertwined that what's good for you is good for me.

In what relationships have you experienced *hesed*? What other verses help you understand the kindness and loyalty God requires of us?

Even when relationships are broken, or when tempers are tried, or when our sense of self-worth is fragile, hesed means we love so much that we go out of our way to make life better for one another. It takes tenderness or kindness to make this happen. In the midst of crazy lives, it takes loyalty and commitment. Hesed requires an intimate knowledge of one another. The requirements of justice are much more general, because things like food, clothing, shelter, companionship, and health are needs that we all share and deserve. But hesed is kindness that comes undeserved, something special that may touch just one single person's life in a special way. Hesed means sticking with people when they are most unlovable and least deserving of special treatment, because of the depth of the bonds between us. Hesed is always the kind of love God has for us, because God loves us when we are least lovable and least deserving. In the same way, hesed is the love we are to have for each other.

Walk humbly with your God serves as the last of Micah's three requirements. It would be better to translate this phrase as walking reverently with God. A healthy self-esteem and a strong sense of self-worth as God's partners are vital parts of what religious life means. Reverence means that we walk with God in worship and in full recognition of how different and holy God is. There is a sense of awe in how we relate to God, because we realize how vast and majestic God is. Our life with God is full of thanksgiving, praise, and worship.

But whether we think of this as walking humbly or as walking reverently with God, it still makes us aware of the need to walk with God and to let God set the agenda for our lives. We are God's partners; God is not our servant. God is moving in directions in the world that were in place long before us and will still be active long after us. We have the privilege of joining with God in these purposes and these activities for a while. We cannot afford the indulgence of thinking in the short-term, or in terms of what we want out of life. God calls us to love the world in order to save it. God invites us to be partners in making this a just world. God asks us to be the body of Christ in the world today, to make God's glory visible to those who have not yet seen God directly. In all these things, we walk with God very closely, following God's lead and living forth God's example.

What other verses help you know how we should walk with God? What things can you do to live this kind of life with God?

3. Examine yourselves 🔑

"EXamine yourselves to see whether you are living in the faith. Test yourselves. Do you not realize that Jesus Christ is in you?" (2 Corinthians 13:5)

In his letter to the church at Corinth, Paul provides his readers with a challenge. Paul frequently explains that we are the body of Christ, and the idea that Jesus is in us is a very central notion in Paul's writing. We are in Christ, just as Christ is in us. We know this through the results of this relationship, as Christ transforms our lives, gives us new priorities, and calls us forward to new ministries for God. In other places, Paul talks specifically about the spirit of Christ that is in us, which produces fruits of the spirit and empowers us to do what is right and good in the world, as God's partners.

ABC's of the Bible

Paul specifically tells the Corinthians—and us—to examine ourselves to see if Christ is in us. We are supposed to test ourselves and look closely at our lives to see the difference that life in Jesus makes. In what ways do our actions provide the proof of God's work in us? These are challenging questions for any of us. As hard as we try, as good as our intentions are, there are always parts of our lives we wish were hidden, even from ourselves. None of us are perfect. Paul does not mean to imply that we should be perfect or that we should have no moral failings.

Sometimes we think of these tests of faith as lengthy tests like we faced in school. Maybe they are true-false tests: "Have you ever had an evil thought?" Or maybe they are multiple choice tests: "Have you ever committed any of the following sins?" This isn't the way God tests us.

A better image comes at the end of the Gospel of John. The story occurs after Jesus' crucifixion and resurrection. Twice earlier, Jesus appeared to his followers. Now, Jesus meets them when they are finishing a morning of fishing. When they return to the shore, Jesus has already cooked them a breakfast of fish. Jesus talks with Simon Peter about feeding his sheep.

Read John 21:15–17.

Here is the only question on Jesus' test, the only thing Paul asks about: Whom do you love? Related questions include: Do you really love Jesus? Do you love the Lord your God with all your heart, soul, and strength? It is the only question that matters. If you do love God, then caring for others and feeding God's sheep comes naturally. All the things Micah says God requires will be obvious because they are part of what you do when you're in love with God. All the instruction of the Torah comes down to this. If you love God, the rest is natural.

Allow time for each person to silently reflect on these questions: Examine yourself and your priorities. Is Christ in you? Do you love God? Do your actions show it? With a new commitment to love God in your heart, what will you do differently?

When Paul tells us to examine ourselves, it's good advice. It's good in any relationship to take an inventory of what we are doing and to ask ourselves if it really expresses true love. Maybe there are habits to break, new habits to begin, and new routines to set.

4. Follow the lighted path

"Your word is a lamp to my feet and a light to my path." (Psalm 119:105)

Psalm 119 is a very long psalm. In fact, it's the longest chapter in any book of the Bible. But it has a very simple, direct theme. God's word and God's law of the Torah are the most important things in life. This verse represents that theme perfectly.

Bible reading is the process of listening to God's word and God's instructions of the Torah. The process is a form of communication with God. Through regular Bible reading, God's path for life becomes clearer. Throughout this study of Bible verses, the Bible should have become more familiar. But there is much more to learn. God's instructions include much more detail about the path God invites us to walk.

Any relationship depends upon good communication and really listening to the one whom we love. We can listen to God through Bible reading and through regular prayer. How will you keep in good communication with God?

How does regular communication with God affect your relationship with the rest of your life? When have you experienced uneasiness in your life, possibly as a result of a lack of communication with God?

5. Climb down the tree

"Zacchaeus, hurry and come down; for I must stay at your house today." (Luke 19:5)

The final Bible verse for this study comes from one of the best known stories of Jesus' preaching and teaching. As Jesus walks through a town, a crowd gathers. Lots of people have come together to see and hear Jesus, but the crowd is so thick that it blocks

CONNECTING WITH LIFE

Discuss how group members can support one another. How will you turn these six sessions into regular patterns of Bible reading? What further study can you do together or individually?

Read Luke 19:7–10.

ABC's of the Bible

the view for many people. One man, named Zacchaeus, climbs a tree so he can get a better view of Jesus over the heads of the crowd. As Jesus walks by, Jesus looks up in the tree, calls Zacchaeus by name, and invites himself to his home.

The crowd isn't happy with this turn of events. They argue that Zacchaeus is hardly the most worthy of them all. He's wealthy, but his gains are all from shady dealings. They suspect Zacchaeus is not a righteous man, and they think Jesus is ruining his own reputation to be with someone like that.

When have you risked your reputation to be with someone that others considered unworthy? How did you cope with what others thought about you?

Jesus seeks out just such people for special attention all throughout the Gospels. Jesus' activity focuses on the people that society thinks are the least. Jesus' term for this is the *reign of God*. Paul calls it the *body of Christ*. Either way, God's people are made up of those whom society rejects, and through these people, God loves the world. Zacchaeus understands this immediately, and he promises to give his money to the needy in order to express God's love. He is not buying Jesus' affection; Jesus has already reached out to Zacchaeus first. Zacchaeus isn't paying back any of his sins; there's no claim that he sinned. Jesus never calls him a sinner; only the crowd does in their rejection of him. Neither guilt nor repentance motivate what Zacchaeus gives away. Instead, his only motive is love—the same love Jesus showed him and that God always lavishes upon the world through Jesus, Zacchaeus, and people like us.

Learning about God is not enough. It is not enough for Zacchaeus to sit in a tree and wait for Jesus to come by so that he could listen and learn. In the same way, it isn't enough for us to study the Bible. As good and as necessary as Bible study is, it is only the beginning of relationship with God. It leads to something else. Bible reading should lead to a deeper relationship with God, a more complete love of God, a more intimate communication with God, and a further commitment to join in partnership with what God is doing in and for the world. Zacchaeus had to come down out of the tree in order to work on a relationship with Jesus and to begin the joyful task of loving the world with Jesus.

For us, there are times to open our Bibles and study. There are times to pray and learn about God through our discussions with each other. There are also times to close our Bibles and give our lives to the loving service of the world. These are both necessary parts of the same faith, the faith to which God calls us through the pages of scripture. Zacchaeus became a follower, a disciple of Christ. We need to do the same.

6. Build your relationship with God

Following Jesus and learning the lessons of scripture mean commitments to discipleship and the discipline of the Christian life. It means taking responsibility for a continuing relationship with God, both in scripture reading and in life with God beyond the pages of the Bible.

There are many ways of regularly practicing reading the Bible. Over the past six sessions, you have studied twenty-six verses and read about many others. What ways of Bible reading and study work best for you?

How many of these twenty-six verses have you memorized? Which ones made an impact on your life? It can help to write them on index cards or use the list on pages 78–79 to refer to throughout the day.

Would it work for you to devote regular time—maybe fifteen minutes a day—to reading scripture by yourself? If so, what time of day will work best for you?

Would it work for you to commit to regular Bible study with the people in your group or with others?

How has the Bible led you to make a change in your life? How has this study helped you connect to God and others?

CONNECTING WITH GOD

Discuss ways of continuing study. How can group members support one another in further study?

If so, schedule that time, and choose another FAITH CROSSINGS resource to help you.

Would something else work better for you? If so, can you help one another find the right way to get closer to scripture? Will you remind one another to stay committed and to keep reading the Bible together?

7. Pray together

Our God,
We praise you because you have spoken to us in the
Bible and in our lives.
We volunteer to be your partners in loving service to
the world.
Please keep our hearts and our minds close to you.
Let your word be in our hearts and on our lips.
May your word be light for our paths.
May we find salvation in the partnership that you
offer.
Guide us in our Bible reading, in our study,
and in our love for you and the world.

Amen.

Pray together in unison.

ENRICHING THE EXPERIENCE

1. Do sorting activities

Ahead of time, use a word processor to create a series of twenty-six cards, each card with a verse from this study, or enlarge on a photocopy machine the verses on pages 78–79. Make a copy of the set for each group member, then cut apart and place each set in an envelope.

At the beginning of this study, group members can use the cards as a tool for memorization or reflection. After completing the study, invite each person to sort through the cards and choose his or her five favorites. Then in pairs or groups of three, group members can compare the reasons they selected these verses as their favorites.

The group as a whole can sort the verses into categories. One person can start a list on newsprint or chalkboard, using these headings: Knowing God, Good Advice, Ethics, and Worship. Group members can work through their decks and call out letters of verses that might apply to each category. The recorder can list the letters under each heading. Afterward, read the verses aloud under each category. What verses were not listed under any category?

Group members can keep their cards to post around their homes or places of work to help them continue memorizing the verses or to refresh their memories.

2. Create artistic expressions

Create an arts experience! As a group, choose one or more of the following ways to express the verses artistically.

▲ Use high-quality paper and calligraphy pens to draw the letters of the verses and create a "miniposter" for each verse. As another option, use a publishing program on a computer to create the posters.

▲ Use clay and sculpt a form that evokes the spirit of a verse.

▲ Set a verse to music, reworking the words as necessary.

▲ Make a quilt-style banner. Each person can illustrate a favorite verse on a block of felt, by gluing or sewing on patches of cloth, or by writing or drawing with fabric paints. Stitch together several blocks to make a quilt banner.

3. Do group research

What questions does the group have about the Bible? Use Bible study tools such as concordances, Bible dictionaries, commentaries, and computer programs to discover possible answers. Or use a concordance (or concordance computer program) to put together a different list of verses than the ones studied in this course.

4. Invite a guest scholar

A Bible scholar or minister with strong biblical skills can visit and make a presentation or have a dialogue about such topics as:

▲ The development of the Bible

▲ An overview of some biblical themes

▲ An evaluation of different biblical translations and paraphrases

▲ A question-and-answer session around questions the group has developed

LIST OF ABC SCRIPTURES

"As for me and my household, we will serve the LORD." (Joshua 24:15b)

"Blessed are the poor in spirit, for theirs is the kingdom of heaven." (Matthew 5:3)

"Create in me a clean heart, O God, and put a new and right spirit within me." (Psalm 51:10)

"Do to others as you would have them do to you." (Luke 6:31)

"Each of you must give as you have made up your mind, not reluctantly or under compulsion, for God loves a cheerful giver." (2 Corinthians 9:7)

"For God so loved the world that he gave his only Son, so that everyone who believes in him may not perish but may have eternal life." (John 3:16)

"Go therefore and make disciples of all nations, baptizing them in the name of the Father and of the Son and of the Holy Spirit, and teaching them to obey everything that I have commanded you. And remember, I am with you always, to the end of the age." (Matthew 28:19–20)

"Hear, O Israel: The LORD is our God, the LORD alone. You shall love the LORD your God with all your heart, and with all your soul, and with all your might." (Deuteronomy 6:4–5)

"In the beginning when God created the heavens and the earth, the earth was a formless void and darkness covered the face of the deep, while a wind from God swept over the face of the waters. Then God said, 'Let there be light'; and there was light." (Genesis 1:1–3)

"Jesus began to weep." (John 11:35)

"Keep straight the path of your feet, and all your ways will be sure." (Proverbs 4:26)

"Let each of you look not to your own interests, but to the interests of others." (Philippians 2:4)

"Mary said, 'My soul magnifies the Lord, and my spirit rejoices in God my Savior.'" (Luke 1:46–47)

"Now faith is the assurance of things hoped for, the conviction of things not seen." (Hebrews 11:1)

"Out of the depths I cry to you, O LORD." (Psalm 130:1)

"Prophesy to these bones, and say to them: O dry bones, hear the word of the LORD. Thus says the Lord GOD to these bones: I will cause breath to enter you, and you shall live." (Ezekiel 37:4)

"Quiet words of the wise are more to be heeded than the shouting of a ruler among fools." (Ecclesiastes 9:17)

"Remember the sabbath day, and keep it holy." (Exodus 20:8)

"Seek the LORD while he may be found, call upon him while he is near." (Isaiah 55:6)

"The spirit of the Lord GOD is upon me, because the LORD has anointed me." (Isaiah 61:1)

"Unless the LORD builds the house, those who build it labor in vain. Unless the LORD guards the city, the guard keeps watch in vain." (Psalm 127:1)

"The Voice of one crying out in the wilderness: 'Prepare the way of the Lord, make his paths straight.'" (Luke 3:4)

"What does the LORD require of you but to do justice, and to love kindness, and to walk humbly with your God?" (Micah 6:8)

"EXamine yourselves to see whether you are living in the faith. Test yourselves. Do you not realize that Jesus Christ is in you?" (2 Corinthians 13:5)

"Your word is a lamp to my feet and a light to my path." (Psalm 119:105)

"Zacchaeus, hurry and come down; for I must stay at your house today." (Luke 19:5)

LOOK FOR THESE
FAITH CROSSINGS TITLES:

Available now:

God's Ordinary People—A look at some fascinating but little-known biblical characters.

Faith Talk—An introduction to basic Christian beliefs.

Following God into the Future—As we welcome a new millennium, where will our faith journeys take us?

Through the Fire—A Bible study on facing tough times.

ABC's of the Bible—Twenty-six key verses draw us into the fascinating world of scripture.

Show No Partiality—A lively dialogue on facing the challenge of racism.

Available June 1999:

Living Water—Take the plunge—Explore the rich symbolism of water in the Bible!

Worship—the Whys, Whats, and Hows—Explore vital questions about what it means to worship God.

Forgiveness—Who Needs It?—In a complex and violent world, where does forgiveness fit in?

Watch for other fascinating FAITH CROSSINGS courses in the future!

To Order: Call Christian Board at 1-800-366-3383.
Visit our Web site: www.cbp21.com

Send your comments about this study to: curriculum@cbp21.com